Where You Are Suppose To Be

GDR

145. pupa the metamorphosis
146. without
147. clearing all of you
148. where you are suppose to be

<u>all the works</u>
I know you might be stressed out
and don't know which way is up
but if you do at least one thing
you love each day
there will always be a little light
so keep wandering
and trust what's within
because the power is you
and nothing is i'mpossible

<u>quiet time</u>
I don't think people realize
when they are in college
that when you live with people
you often are alone
and having to do deal with issues
that may help you when you have a family

I think people are afraid of living alone
to be alone with one's thoughts
to enjoy one's own company

<u>overthinking I</u>
I have been overthinking lately
about my weight
how I look
if I am doing well in school
it is just this constant wall that I run into
again and again
sometimes I can break through
and other times
I fall flat on my ass

<u>street lights</u>
the drifts of snow cover my windshield and
slide off effortlessly in the wind
the white lights guide the road ahead of me

<u>sore throat</u>
I took a break from writing
just about a week
and I felt the side affects
a brain with clumps of information
with nowhere to set them down
events have occurred
and I lost my voice in the noise

<u>sold the soul</u>
I see these shops with jewelry lining the
walls and am reminded by
what I use to create
my family says my stuff should be up there
but my work was tainted
trying to please others with what I made
I lost sight of my enjoyment
the only difference between my jewelry and
poetry is that I don't care if people like my
poems
I write for the sole purpose of passing along
what I have learned to my children
a record to look back on
something tangible for when I am long gone

<u>who are you</u>
who are you when you are all alone
are you who you want to be
and if so
why not show the world your colors
because there is someone out there that
wants to see you paint the canvas
and awe at the details of your life
don't let society lower the texture of you
don't let society change your details

<u>just a few things</u>
the smell of rain
the gloom of the clouds that makes staying
inside under a blanket okay to do

the day after a good snow when the sun is
out and the snowballs are perfect

the morning of weekends when grass is
freshly cut and it smells like game day

the evenings when you wave goodbye to a
sleepy sun

the late nights when caffeine keeps up the
ghostly to watch the stars shine for them

that feeling of a swollen heart with too much
love to contain

just a few things I love about this life

<u>dear body</u>
I am sorry
for being to harsh on you lately
for criticizing you when
I should be cherishing you
you are a vessel that allows me to do
wondrous things
you have more miles on you than the car I
drive
you have scars that are proof
of your perseverance
sometimes when I look in the mirror I don't
like what I see
when it is you that has given me
the opportunity to take each day in stride
I am sorry I have not been there
but I am here now

<u>made to reach</u>
you are more than you know
you are made from the dust of galaxies
the fire of the sun beats in you
all these atoms course through the fabric of
your being
and yet you are a spec that
looks to the stars
chases them
builds toward them

<u>numerical value</u>

why do we let grades define
who our children are
the representation of knowledge holds no
number value
the representation of knowledge is the
mastery of skills
anyone can study for an exam and memorize
the material
but to show knowledge in everyday life
is what we should show our children
that knowledge is power
not some gpa
not a number
but value and purpose

<u>a diamond made from coal</u>
I am strong because I have failed
I and soft in a world that is hard
in a storm I will remain calm
I am light in the shadows

<u>overthinking II</u>

I judge myself harder than I should
I push myself into the dirt as
I try to be better but continue to fail
there is a guilt of failure that I feel
and sometimes I cannot push it away

<u>the tea shop</u>
I remember those nights
we sat in your car and just talked
it's as if you were suppose
to drive me home
I do not resent meeting you
I still have the photo of you
from our first date
and hope you are doing well

<u>locks have changed</u>
you come to me on your timetable
when it is easy for you
not asking how I am or anything
just meaningless   I miss you
and empty   let's get together
pushing your luck with my heart strings
making a caring person cold
I've tried expressing how I feel
and setting ground rules on what I need
and instead of meeting half way
I get half-assed lies
and not so sorry sorrys
you're just not listening
and I'm done wasting my breath
you can try coming to
my door and knocking
but the locks have changed
since you last showed

<u>no place</u>
you have dwelled in shame long enough
it is time to let go of what you regret
move on and grow

<u>sails at your back</u>
what would happen if you
couldn't do what you loved
to be an empty vessel in the
middle of the ocean
no compass

be thankful for the sails at your back
and use what you do to better this world

<u>little pieces of me</u>
I put my soul into these words
extract them like sap from a tree
just to watch them pour onto these pages
and it's funny how a manmade language can
be so powerful
to tear down faster than a sword
or build up like a hammer

<u>envious</u>
find the people who don't find the light
within you intimidating

<u>cutting the string</u>
I can feel your energy
tugging on the severed string
that bound us
you are probably upset with me
but I had to put myself first when
I was used as your battery

<u>just a shell of an old landscape</u>
these words bottle up like a volcano
threatening to explode
they weigh heavy on my chest
but all I know is that the lava
that erupts from my core
adds new layers to my soul
purifying the ground only few walk on
allowing flowers of all variety's to sprout
in my rib cage
because who am I
without
the emotions
the glances
the words

just a shell of an old landscape

<u>1-22-21</u>

I guess I am writing to my future self
tonight was a wonderful night spent with the
most important people in your life
it flew by in a blink
and so I am telling you to savor the
moments with people you love
life moves so fast and we forget all the
beautiful moments spent

<u>cut short</u>
do we truly plan the end
what happens to all those plans
all those experiences
all those sunsets
all those books
all those laughs
yet to happen
what about the people
we were suppose to meet

<u>deserve what is served</u>
I am here to show you an
old sentimental love
something that is few and far
between these days
you may think that you deserve
what is being served to you
I disagree
you deserve the world
and hopefully someday
you will realize you
deserve nothing less
and one day someone
will give you it

<u>oh the future</u>
I am walking into a forest
a crescent moon above me
the earth below me
and a path yet to be carved
into this dark tapestry
I have constellations guiding me
and my soul inside me
at first it seems intimidating
but oh
how the future feels exhilarating

<u>blunt</u>
I don't write pretty
or count syllables
or try to rhyme even though it happens often
to me that is all fluff
and life could give a shit if you're okay
I want my words to be straight as an arrow

<u>radiance of twilight</u>
you do not need the sun to grow
you have the moon and her stars

<u>seeking validation</u>
my art is mine
but when it is put on social media
it feels as though a piece is taken away
that this feeling of needing likes
gives me validation
when it is all a lie

<u>overthinking III</u>

when you have something perfectly under
control
and you're trying to relax with friends or
watch a movie or read
that is when it hits
the cranking and turning of the mind
pulling you out of the moment
and digging a hole to throw you in to
sometimes you can climb out
other times you keep slipping

<u>cosmic shower</u>
when my stars felt further away
and the darkness was too quiet
showers came
in brilliant reds and blues
with soft pinks and greens
enough to make a rainbow jealous
and after that breath
I felt closer to the ones I love
they fill my heart past the brink
and make it hard to breath
as that love pours into my lungs

<u>lovely sounds</u>
I use to get irritated from the noise caused
by family members
but as I am living alone
I realize the sound was lovely
that empty space I feel in the mornings is
peaceful but not homey
it is the little things that
I'm realizing were big
my parents stocking up on food
my dads cooking
my moms interruptions from
work to say hey
my dogs barking for attention

<u>words from vision</u>

they say grief is just love with no place to go
and as I move to the next chapter of my life
where I don't see my family as much
the would be hugs and quality time
with them
leaves a hole in my heart

<u>physical storage</u>
our bodies store so much wisdom
they hold emotions
of what isn't said
they boil over burning the skin
when they have had enough
your throat may hurt from
all the words left unsaid
your shoulders may hurt from
the burden you believe you should carry
you may be taking shallow
breaths from the pain of grief
your stomach may be tight
from the stress you hold in
our bodies hold us up
but be sure you let out all the things you feel

<u>warmth in a cold world</u>
be brave enough to try
it doesn't matter what you
look like or believe
show the world your pure heart

<u>fall far from the tree</u>
do not place blame on a group based off a
few bad apples
some are trying to change the world despite
being placed in the basket of bad apples

<u>the list goes on</u>
we worry about things that aren't apart of
the big picture
focused on how we look on paper
versus how we are as a human being
focused on our cracked
smiles in insta stories
and not looking deeper to heal
focused on the next high
and not in the moment
focused on how to use people
for our own benefit
and not finding those who
make us better
focused on talking
not listening
the list goes on

<u>grief</u>
I feel like a tree
full of leaves
with wet snow dangling on my
branches trying to bring me down
and with this weight I cannot breath
instead I am brought to the ground
but maybe the earth is trying to tell me to
hold on to my roots
because change is afoot

<u>freshly plastered</u>
to the places we search for all our lives
no selfies or panoramic photos
can take in the beauty
our memories rise like film freshly
plastered on file
but please don't let it face the sun
or the picture could be tarnished
let these places or people
simmer in you mind
and await for those
feelings of a happy memory

<u>take a break</u>

your mind is on a tightrope with no safety
as it travels to the future
take a breath
you've been holding it in too long
the lactic acid is building up in your muscles
stretch to show your body appreciation
for all the places it takes you
learn to love
love yourself not for your strength but for
your weaknesses
to love others in a world
shielded from warmth
let your soul fly
and see everything from the perspective of
the clouds
take a break
there is no time limit
you'll go when you're ready

<u>black mirrors</u>
connected to the outlet on my wall
the screens that light up everywhere
the endless screens
it's time to look outside
to connect with the outlets in the soil
the trees stand still everywhere
endless trees

<u>life is</u>
life is the laughs
it's the hugs you never want to end
and the moments that pass too quickly
it's the smell of the rain on concrete
and the sound of a rushing river
it's the first bloom of spring
and the last leaf changing in fall
it's the kisses and I love you's
it's the sunsets
that look too beautiful to be real
it's getting lost to become found
it's the growing old without what ifs
it's messy
it's wonderful
it's full of light in all dark corners

<u>overthinking IV</u>
I plan ahead to free my mind
but sometimes it makes it worse
it's like trying to make the wind flow in my
direction
when the wind moves freely
so instead of moving along
I gasp for air as it rushes into my face

<u>a letter to a past life</u>
I understand times were different
I have no idea what it must have been like
400 years ago taking orders to stay alive
society built on an awful system with unjust
people
you just happened to fall into the trap
the people you hurt have forgiven you
and moved on
if they haven't
I have already forgiven them for you
the only thing I need you to do is forgive
yourself
I guess we both have the same problem
but let's work through this together
the past is the past
we have learned
you have given me the skills
to be better in this life
so let go of the shackles you have placed on
yourself and know you have been blessed

<u>old friends</u>
I still have ties to you
I still think about you from time to time
wondering what it would be like if you
didn't shut me out and come beg
when I stopped knocking
I hope you are doing well
and are safe and happy
I'm writing to let you know I am cutting the
cord and moving on
there is no need to have you on my
shoulders any longer
may god bless you and stay well

<u>fill the rabbit hole</u>
I hope you know everything is okay
you do not need to be so hard on yourself
stop digging deeper and
climb out to the light

<u>a canvas</u>
my body is a canvas
etched with scars that showcase
my trials and tribulations
carved with wrinkles from laughing
emotion dashed with ink
this ink is a visual reminder that
I have my
mom
dad
brother
and God
with me
my mom and dad look over
my shoulder and back
they have been my protectors and teachers
my brother is on my right arm
my strong side as he is my best friend
I have God on my left
guiding the words I write on this very page

<u>legacy</u>
at the end of all things what will
you leave behind
will your love live on in your children
will your words echo in a dusty book
waiting to be found
or are we just a segment on the news
with three day coverage
and then tossed aside for the next new thing
I have to believe my life
is a ripple in a pond
a continual motion of love as it passes
I want my children to read my words
to know who I was
to know my voice and how it has matured
how I have grown to become their father
that is why I write
too many times great people pass on
without passing along their thoughts
their own little world dies
I want my words to be the world I have lived
pages upon pages of what I have learned and
how I see this world

law of attraction
we become what we attract
we send energy out into this universe
and the universe responds
because everything has intention
everything has energy
the worlds are connected
to form a solar system
just as people are connected
to form a community
nothing is without purpose
nothing is without energy
once you know this
your whole life will shift
to one of gratefulness
to one of perspective

<u>eagle</u>

I do not need to rush
go dive head first
I will glide
and let the wind carry me to
the right place at the right time
I am not in a rush
no need to chase
looking for the people
searching endlessly
forcing something that isn't there
I will fly
soak up the clouds and the moon
continually trying to be the best me
to believe in myself and love myself
so when everything falls into place
I'll be ready
I am the wind
but forever living on through
the echo of the trees

<u>no matter who notices</u>
a seed fights through the soil to sprout
a mountain defies gravity to reach the stars
the ocean crashes just to pick itself up again
the stars send light from light years away
the moon is shy but will always have a
dance with the earth
the sun paints when it dies and is reborn
and no matter who notices
these things will continue
just as you should
be who you are
always
more will look at you in awe if you do

<u>what we are</u>
find something that will listen without
judgement
not someone
something
these pages accept my thoughts
for what they are and not
what they should be
there is no sound
no judgement
but freedom at the stroke of a pen
you can find a listener
in the pavement you run on
the weights you lift
the car you drive
the art you create

with these listeners
our truest selves are born

<u>a world of wonder</u>
we fear the unknown
no matter what degree this fear holds
it is a primal instinct
to be locked in the dark of
unknown surroundings
this can be what it is like
to try something new
little do we know that within this darkness
our bodies adapt and we change and grow
and soon enough our inner light turns on
in the darkness of change
we fear the unknown
it is a primal instinct
but the unknown unlocks
freedom of self
trust of self
love of self
it is the first step into a world of wonder

<u>climb out</u>
have enough self love
not to be swept under the rug
you're not meant to be stepped on

<u>look for approval</u>
the moon does not apologize for her curves
she chooses how she wants to be
and her emotions range
but never does she look for approval
nor will I
I will try my damnedest
not to apologize
for who I am
nor will I look for the approval in others
it may not happen always
but it is a start

<u>beyond the page</u>
there is so much more to You than the
perspectives written in the book
so much more
You are something that is intangible
but encompasses all things
You are light and love
that fuel the life force of Your creations
no amount of words written will reach
all that You do
whether they choose to
believe or not
You are beyond

<u>self made prisons</u>
we live in cages
self made
by the things we possess
but more by the things we want
open the lock
and step outside
to unlock and dampen the ego
we need to step outside
and be one with nature
where we belong

<u>embers</u>
you are walking art
traversing this strange land
making flowers bloom as you pass
there is light in you
a never ending spark
igniting the shadows on this
side of the universe
your energy radiates
please do not confine your spirit
you have something this world needs to see

<u>the idea of reincarnation strikes as unholy</u>
it raises questions of why suffer through
pain on earth again and again
I do not have data to prove if it is true or not
all I know is that this world is constantly
filled with hatred and prejudice
God may be omnipotent
but only to those whose hearts are open to
His grace
everyone is a child of God and heaven is our
home
I will continue to come back to this earth if
it means I can save a soul
I might suffer from the hatred of men
but oh how I will live
I will be a raindrop cascading through
filthy waters only to purify with my light
I am an agent of God
a physical reminder to those
who have lost their way
that they are loved
there may be a holy book
but God is more than those mere pages
He transcends this space and time
only waiting for our minds
to unlock His secrets

<u>no passport needed</u>
they say to travel the world
to visit places where history speaks
to see and experience other cultures
to dive into exploration
this world has been razed by man
there are barely any places untouched by
mankind
with this said
why not explore the islands
of your own mind
to climb the mountains
and swim in the oceans of your heart
because at the end of the trip
all you'll have is yourself
and I think that is beautiful

<u>internal tides</u>

waves of the past come rushing through
like a stream of memories
it seems as though the past comes to the
forefront when the future is
ready and waiting
in these moments there is a choice
to allow the past to swallow us
or swim to the edge of the river
and walk to the new shore

<u>thank you</u>
I remember all the moments with you
good and bad
I thank you for all you taught me
I hope you are doing well and have found
someone who loves you for who you are
you deserve it

<u>not to impress</u>
trees grow up not to impress others
but to reach their goal
to meet the sun and all her glory
to shed the toxic waste this life has to offer
to carry through the weight of the elements
and laugh with the breeze through the leaves
trees grow up to become the best version of
themselves

<u>phoenix</u>
have you seen the fire coursing
through your veins
the energy flowing and bursting
at the seams
let all of it out
don't contain your fire
for fire can be beautiful and
birth life from destruction
it might burn but oh how you'll feel alive

spring cleaning
back to my roots
finding my zen and refurbishing
my inner peace
it is time to redecorate
my mind and soul are evolving
and with that comes change
to store the old needed condition
and to build new habits of happiness
construction is ever flowing in
this journey
and rightfully so
without flow
there would be nothing

letters to my past

I see you

I hear you

I know I have gone back to look

which has made me fall into despair

overthinking about all

the mountains I have climbed

in my path to loving myself

I look back at them and feel

empty and nervous

I do not need that energy

my friends who have become ghosts

and taught me lessons of strength

do not have the power to

control my emotions

I clear and let go of the past

for I am different than

who I was 4 years ago

I am evolving and with that comes a

past that has shaped me

I thank you for teaching me

I turn that dark emotion and cast it out

into the cosmos asking for

love and happiness

then move on

<u>self love in progress</u>
I have been critiquing my body
blaming it for being hurt for something out
of it's control
you are the vessel that allows me to live
you are my castle
I should be building you up
not tearing you down

<u>not an uber</u>
you are driving you're own life
no need for backseat drivers
you choose where to go
when to stop and when to get gas
how loud the music is
and if the windows are down
stop giving others the power over the wheel
tell them to put a seatbelt on and either
enjoy the ride or to get out of the car

<u>underground railroad</u>
humans have created escape routes
but the truth is
we do not need them
to find nirvana
to get away from a reality we don't like
escaping isn't the answer
connecting with your own soul
to be brave enough to connect
to change your reality
all you need is you

<u>x-ray vision</u>

there are some people who can
see emotions
behind brick and stone
the walls built up to hide
from the outside world are merely glass
no words need to be explained
when energy is given off
and when I can't form the words
or have lost sight
they are the ones who send out a buoy
they are the ones who hold me up
without even touching me
they are otherworldly

<u>chance and circumstance</u>
some do not believe in soul mates
they say it is just a matter of
chance and circumstance
but how can
something so eloquent
something so extraordinary
be by chance
some things are destined
and no matter the time you meet
you will always be steered toward them

<u>nothing of note to say</u>
I have been holding out on writing because
I have thought that I don't have anything
poetic to say
and what a shame that is
because to have a voice in any medium
whether it's through
words
paint
sports
to be brave enough to show yourself
to the world is poetic
it doesn't matter how
pretty you sound or look
all that matters is how you feel
while in the act
and chances are if you do
others will too

<u>do or do not</u>

please try not to run towards the things you
can't have
in doing so you turn a cold shoulder
to those who give you warmth
to those who are there
believe me
turning your back on people you love
to try and have something that isn't yours
only hurts both parties

<u>repeat this</u>
I am enough
I know I am not perfect
and never will be
all that matters is that I try
to be the best version of
myself everyday
and soon
I will find the right people
to grow and learn with
I may already know them
and if I don't
they are out there
I will be patient
I will be open minded
I am a rock the world has
tried to smash only to become
softer amidst the rubble

<u>lights out</u>
I use to run from fear
until I started lifting weights
I got this aesthetic of strength
to hide my fear
always fighting the fear
until I gained more knowledge
to know when to be calm
and when to stand up

<u>the lesson</u>
acknowledging the lesson
and understanding the lesson
are two very different things
the former is mid lesson
when things may be tough and
the realization of learning is at hand
the latter is the frustration
of the toughness without explanation
it isn't until the end that most realize why
past events unfolded as such

<u>no forbidden fruit</u>
love is not the simple and effortless
connection
that will simply grow without work
love is the messy entanglement of weeds
amongst a garden
there is constant care and watering
sometimes weeding is done
and others planting
the effort put in can lead
to the garden of eden
with no forbidden fruit

<u>more value</u>
I give away all my confidence
and all my strength at the flip of a switch
their words
their opinions
cut at my knees and I let it happen
I let their thoughts persuade mine

I need to stop allowing other's thoughts
to enter my mind so freely
no matter who implants them
I must fortify my knees
to endure
to stand tall in my belief
to guard against my confidence
to allow criticisms or judgements
to simply flow like the river
I can sit on the side and not be pulled
in by the current

letters to you
you have come so far
all the obstacles you have faced
the storms you've driven through
all have led you to this point
I know time has gone by fast
and you feel as though you haven't
cherished everything as
much as you've wanted to
you might feel guilty for some decisions
but look back at all the decisions you could
have made but decided to stick it out
and continue to become who you are
I am so proud of you
your patience and determination
has paid off
when times change in the future
please remember where you came from
and all the people who are in your corner

<u>you</u>
your skin doesn't determine who you are
your soul does that
your hard work does that
your brain doesn't think that

<u>crt</u>
the schools cannot decide that
all whites are bad
all blacks are chained
and everything in between is thrown out

coin toss

all of you have been coming
back into my mind
as if making sure I'm cleared before I take
the next steps of my journey
I wonder if you all think I left
because I didn't care
I wonder if you all think I am the bad guy
and if you do that is okay
but please know I tried
I tried to make things work
I held on when I was suffocating
I held on to a ledge that simply didn't exist
trying to run into the light of an
endless tunnel
I had hope for all the good
I thought you were
and I'm not mad for being tossed aside
I still believe you can change
maybe I was the spark to your phoenix
I hope you all have a happy life
but please don't try to hurt me in
my memories

<u>be still</u>

allow me to learn the art of stillness in a
world that is anything but

<u>my experience</u>
lately when I am out and about
I've felt self conscious
hoping not to run into people I know
and how stupid that has been
to not live my life for fear of
seeing somebody

I know who I am and what I've done to get
to this point in my life
I don't need any validation
nor do I need to feel anxious
about people I use to know judging me
I am who I am and if they can't take it
then good riddance
I'm done feeling self conscious in public
and will no longer allow fear to diminish my
experience

<u>the wolf and three pigs</u>
my heart is building a house of cards
and my mind is a little gust of wind

<u>random acts of kindness</u>
I think it is beautiful to compliment
on someone's hair
or clothes
or tattoos
because some just need a little light
I think it's beautiful to comment
about a butterfly flying by
about the sky
about the colors of trees
because the little things can be
so overshadowed
I think it's beautiful to feel
the rain my skin
the ground beneath me
your hand in mine

<u>the process of growth</u>
when planting a seed and watching it grow
we do not judge the process
you don't get mad at the plant for how
it looks when it blooms
you continue to encourage it and water it
nature is perfect just as it is
so the next time you go to judge your body
for not being in perfect shape
just remember the seed

<u>tethered</u>
he is holding out
looking for where he is suppose to land
but is tethered to where he is
little does he know that
he is suppose to figure out why
he is tethered before he can jump

<u>far beyond this place</u>
you can strip away my bone
you can take my organs
break my heart
cut my skin
it's only a vessel of my soul
my thoughts
my emotions
my love
extend far beyond this plane
and cannot be brought down
my soul flies with the moon
drifting in God's endless wind
and if you listen closely
He will speak

<u>good ole days</u>
some might say these years
define you and are where you change
I disagree
I have defined myself
I have found myself
this is merely a stepping stone to my goal

<u>your choice</u>
you are not tethered to anything you haven't
signed up for
it is your life and your time
if something is wasting time or
causing too much stress
then stop it
your first priority is you
and if you are being guilt tripped
they sure as hell don't deserve you

<u>one hello away</u>
how can we say not to talk to strangers
when we are only one introduction
away from meeting
a mentor
a friend
a partner
a guide
it is exhilarating thinking about how you're
one hello away from finding
what you didn't expect

<u>you deserve more</u>
find someone who stimulates your brain
someone who wants to get to know you
for who you are
not some artificial bullshit
the real thing
so many times
people act like they want to get to know you
but it's just because they
want something from you
don't let people leach off your soul
you deserve more
you deserve genuine people
and they are out there
and don't worry
they are looking for you as well

<u>angels landing</u>
I love the days when the sun reaches past the
clouds with a incandescent glow

<u>lost in a trance</u>
there are events in the human experience
that are completely captivating
it can be playing a sport
painting or dancing
or listening to that one song

find those moments
capture them in your
mind's eye

<u>wash over</u>
let love wash over you
you may not have a lot of things
but you have people
people who care for you
you may not feel of value
but without you
the people you've touched
for better or for worse
wouldn't be who they are without you
you're a small drop in a pond
that ripples
let that wash over you

<u>hold on</u>
you define your life
you find your purpose
that is such a powerful thing
so grab it by the reins

<u>millions of drops per second</u>
I forgot the smell of rain on pavement
the simplicity of it
the life it gives
the smile it carves
weightless words

infinite worlds
walking among us are perspectives
we have never seen
ideas we've never thought to think up
heroes in our villains
villains in our heroes
a whole world waiting
to be tread by the right person
deserts in need of rain
oceans that could drown stars
new trails to be paved
mountains to be climbed
all in these people you may
never see again

finding family

some are lucky to find family
within their blood
others find family in strangers
neither is right or wrong
it is just different
but if you're able to find family
you are one lucky soul
hold onto them

<u>to end up here</u>
what are you but a miracle
a mixture of star dust
constantly pumping life through
the galaxy in your veins
what are you but a miracle
facing the world head on
even when you get knocked down
you come back stronger
what are you but a miracle
to end up here
right here with me

<u>not alone</u>
today may have been a good day
today may have been a bad day
all I know is you're here now
and that somewhere out there
someone also had a good day
someone also had a bad day
just know you're not alone

<u>time travel</u>
find the people that take away your worry
even if it's just for an hour
you deserve a break from your own mind

<u>sociology class</u>
some say life isn't determined
it is all free will
others say everything is already destined
I believe life is a tree
and you start where you'd like to begin
whether it's a branch or a leaf
and as you make decisions
you run along your path
it can take you anywhere along the tree
but it always ends at the trunk of the tree
no matter where the journey takes you
you always end up where you belong

<u>dear matty</u>
it is almost that time of year again
I hope you know sometimes I see you
roaming our house and just sniffing around
I haven't forgotten about you
I know gabby misses you
and won't let mya in because of it
maybe you can help her clear that
so she can become close with mya
I know you're up in heaven running around
but feel free to visit anytime you'd like

due date blues

I am not a chegg subscription
giving out answers whenever you're stuck
lazy enough not to do it yourself
or when you wait until the last minute
I have more value than that
I am a teacher
to explain my faults and hope you decide
what is best for you
but if you think of me as an afterthought
a slave to your procrastination
you're dead wrong
because I have more value than that

<u>transplant</u>

don't forget your roots
no thing can grow without them
don't take them for granted
because when you move on
there will be a void that is hard to fill

<u>revival</u>
I feel so strong in their presence
like anything is conquerable
I get to retreat and rest
with them

<u>meet where you are</u>
we hold onto so much
expectations of
our jobs
our families
our schooling
our sports
our bodies
our abilities
our friends
that it seems as though the whole world is
on our shoulders
but little do we know that we can set the
globe down
and roll with it
and start by meeting ourselves for
where we are
and live by the goals and values
for what we define them as

<u>the fleeting moment</u>
always looking toward the next task
always looking down at a screen
always doing something
chasing someone
running from someone
that we miss this moment
to stop and stare at a sunrise
or watch the clouds roll by

<u>self destruction</u>
I can be my own worst enemy
pushing myself towards the flame of hatred
verbally beating myself up
when I don't meet a number
whether it be
a percent on a test
the weight on a scale
as long as I put my best foot forward then
there is no way I can't succeed
I can succeed through failure
no number can define happiness
no number can value worth

<u>visas</u>

we are escapists
looking to feel apart of something bigger
only to realize it is just as lonely

<u>sharing the same sky</u>
someone is out there for you
someone is hoping for you
someone is restless for you and it might
seem like a big world with few possibilities
but maybe you are sharing the
same stars at night
inching closer in alignment
with each passing day
until the moment when you're both ready

<u>goes both ways</u>
you don't realize how much you're helping
someone when you're the one being helped
but it is a double sided coin
in receiving help you
are strengthening
the other

<u>so be</u>
what we do resembles
what we are
our actions come from emotions
our thoughts come from external actions
our art is our blood
and our blood is made up of fragments from
the universe
humans are so diverse
so intelligent and gentle
so be who you are
the world needs your art
but some do not deserve it

<u>from within</u>
all the answers are within
it just depends how deep you're willing to
go in search of your purpose

<u>a gift</u>
you have a chance to live today
to feel something
to change
to grow

wind beneath me
I will land where I need to
I may not know how or where or when
but I shall reach my destination
I know this because I walk with Him
He is my guide
He is the wind beneath my wings

<u>moon lotion</u>
a couple months ago I didn't know anybody
now I got this dude I see everyday
he makes college less lonely
and more tolerable
and I'm thankful he
appeared in my life

<u>pain of living</u>

people ask why would you get a tattoo if
they hurt and last forever
my only response is that
anything meaningful in this life causes pain
and will be with you forever
going through each day
there will be pain
but we still live
we choose to live
so why not showcase what is
meaningful to us
what keeps us going

<u>nan-tan</u>
I saw a meteorite burn up
and sizzle down to earth
not 20 yards from me
I was tempted to go look
for it while I was driving
but it was so unexpected
I didn't even make a wish
some things are so spontaneous that no
camera could capture
so look up
or you might miss it

<u>who to trust</u>
this world has faulty information thrown
around like the weather forecast
except some of the information
isn't as benign as the weather

<u>mysterio</u>
the strongest people can be tricked into
seeing something that isn't there
and sometimes the fog is too thick to escape
and who they once were can be lost forever

<u>shape sorting</u>
it's funny you know
we grow up and learn
and are taught we are more
than just a grade
and then those same teachers stamp
a letter on sheets of paper to represent our
knowledge
when there are so many other
factors to describe intelligence
every day we are calculating
calories we eat and burn
time to do our work
how much money we have for the week
how many days until the weekend
but some things are incalculable
your warmth
your heart
your conscience
your intelligence
just because you're good at taking a test
doesn't mean you know the material
don't let the world define you based on its
naive constructs
you fit outside the box

<u>click bait</u>
many times the grass on
the other side is just astro turf
the sugar is switched with the salt
the frosting is all that looks good
the cover is super cool
all it is is bait
to entice
to hook you on
and take the oxygen from your lungs
there is always more than meets the eye
and sometimes when the mind
fails to recognize it
it is the gut feeling that
can make or break you
so hold on to how you feel
the answers are hidden beneath

<u>a dedication to you</u>
I saw an old teacher of mine today
probably the only teacher I'd ever want to
go back and visit with
when it comes to writing
he started a fire within me
I'll always be grateful for that
when I saw him the good memories
of middle school which
were few and far between
came back
he was always there for me
and seeing his face light up made
my day so special
I hope he knows how
much he impacted me

<u>when I'm old</u>
to say you saw the opening night
of some amazing films
to your children will be so special
when you rewatch it with them

<u>so grow and soar</u>
there is no need to be trapped in a cage
to feel as though there is no way out
to feel as though you belong there
your situation is what you make it to be
not as it once was
time is constantly changing
and so are you
so grow
be who you're meant to be
your unconscious freedom
will lead your conscience
to fly through the bars of this plane
to soar

<u>my mama</u>
she is so strong
so brave
to want to give to people
who are so self centered
so dreadful to be around
and yet she doesn't let
her heart become hard
she is soft
she cries when blows are taken
but she keep getting up to help
I don't understand it
constantly in pain
but trying to help
I guess that's just what being
a mother is all about

<u>lost sight</u>
I've been in his shoes before
been blinded by a love
and not seeing the pain
it causes those around
when they say love is blind
it truly is
and it can be the most destructive
thing on this earth

<u>my dream catcher</u>
you have always supported me
told me you'll hold the space for me
you are my protector from bad dreams
and my teacher in the art of spirituality
you have always welcomed
going to rock shops
and delving into the chakras with me
I thank you

<u>dusting the cobwebs</u>
I feel confident again in putting
myself out there to meet people
there was a period where we all
didn't have the chance to
and I think it made me rusty

space itself is expanding
in a world so disconnected
so hungry for power
with empathy for nothing and no one
where do you stand
among the crowd
or are you the little bit of warmth
scattered across the stars
shining
but so far away
I don't blame you
it hurts to be in the present
over loaded with
emotions and thoughts of
the past and future colliding
expected to do so much
either from your peers
or just your own high standards
just know that not all of your todos or goals
need to be completed today
you can relax and have a life

<u>masked up</u>
it is so hard to get to know
those around me
to actually make
connections in a masked world
literally
and figuratively

<u>I'm my own carver</u>
I use to be bullied about
my weight
my feet
my height
the way I dressed
even things that weren't wrong with me
just to get under my skin
to shove me down
but little do they know
these trials
shaped who I am today
they tried to make me crack under pressure
but instead made me soft in a world so cold

<u>overthinking V</u>
I overthink
that problem on the test
the way I said something
how someone looked at me
how people speak to me
I overthink
not because I mean to
not because I want to
my brain is just constantly
on the move
I overthink
all the reasons why I do something
all the reasons why I like or dislike
something
I've thought of them
I overthink and that is just a part of
who I am

<u>right timing is a myth</u>
things occur at the time we do not choose
as soon as we stop searching
for what we want or need
it finds its way to us
right underneath our noses

<u>immersive</u>
the sun kissed our backs
as wind blew threw the trees
each rock with its own subtleties
so quiet
to respect nature
and be one with it
is a different level of climbing

<u>scenic route</u>

we are here for such a short time

it's okay to take detours

it's okay to look out the windows

<u>the search</u>
everything is born with purpose
the cool thing about being human is
that we get to find and define ours

<u>wouldn't be me</u>
I was reminiscing about you tonight
I do not regret the time I had with you
when you opened up to me
what we had was kind and beautiful
you were my first for a lot of things
you showed me so much
you taught me so much
I am so thankful for all that you
brought into my life
I hope you are doing what you love
and have found people who love you for
who you are

<u>the uno reverse of life</u>
we all take the tests life offers first
and then we learn the lessons

<u>sounds of spring</u>
walking along a concrete path
realizing that beyond the hustle bustle
of man made todos
the birds speak to each other
in such beautiful melodies
and we are rarely able to hear them

<u>fist bump</u>
to know he feels the same
about our friendship
how we've made an impact on one another
in such a short time
not being able to fathom what this year
would've been like had we not gotten to
know each other
just makes me believe
our paths were meant to cross

<u>fear of drowning</u>
life is like the sea
with such vastness
calming waters
showered by storms
and I only scratch the
surface of it while in my boat
so I dive
deep as I can go
and would drown a thousand times over
if it means that I lived

<u>pupa the metamorphosis</u>
my heart is trapped in my chest
or maybe my rib cage is it's cocoon
ready to open up and be the wings
to my fleeing heart
it is in search of you
and it will fly around the world
to get to you

<u>without</u>
what is life without art
what is art without life
there is nothing without one or the other
living brings out all shades and hues
and art adds to the feelings of life

<u>clearing all of you</u>
my memories of some people are fleeting
moments of happiness
my wanting of love from those
who couldn't even help themselves
I am thankful for all of them
for showing me that I can give myself love
and that quantity doesn't mean quality
I wish you all well
and thank you

<u>where you are suppose to be</u>
this life has no wrong paths
some are carved in stone
others a foot wide trail amongst tall grass
don't let anyone persuade you
from your path
it isn't theirs to walk
do not feel the need to be as far ahead as
your peers
otherwise you'll miss the lessons
only you need
this moment embarks
the rest of your life
and guess what
you are right
where you are suppose to be

check out these other books

wanderer - 2018

from within - 2018

I'mpossible - 2019

the power is you - 2020

a little light - 2021

about the author

garrett risdon is a 20 year old writer who
has delved into poetry for the last four
years

he loves the outdoors including hiking
and paddle boarding

garrett attends colorado state university
and is currently studying
civil engineering

Made in the USA
Monee, IL
19 July 2022

99973501R00089